Book of Dreams

By Enoch

Copyright © 2020 Lamp of Trismegistus. All rights reserved. No part of this publication may be reproduced or transmitted in any form or by any means, electronic or mechanical, including photocopying, recording, or by any information storage and retrieval system, without permission in writing from Lamp of Trismegistus. Reviewers may quote brief passages.

ISBN: 978-1-63118-437-6

Christian Apocrypha Series

Other Books in this Series and Related Titles

The Testament of Abraham by Abraham (978-1-63118-441-3)

The Book of Astronomical Secrets by Enoch (978-1-63118-443-7)

Psalms of Solomon by King Solomon (978-1-63118-439-0)

The Lives of Adam and Eve by Moses (978-1-63118-414-7)

The First and Second Gospels of the Infancy of Jesus Christ by Thomas and James (978-1-63118-415-4)

Lost Chapters of the Book of Daniel and Related Writings by Daniel (978-1-63118-417-8)

The Testament of Moses by Moses (978-1-63118-440-6)

The Book of the Watchers by Enoch (978-1-63118-416-1)

The Book of Parables by Enoch (978-1-63118-429-1)

Masonic Symbolism of Easter and the Christ in Masonry by various authors (978-1-63118-434-5)

A Few Masonic Sermons by A. C. Ward & Bascom B. Clarke (978-1-63118-435-2)

Masonic Symbolism of King Solomon's Temple by Albert G. Mackey & others (978-1-63118-442-0)

Cloud Upon the Sanctuary by A. E. Waite & K. Eckartshausen (978-1-63118-438-3)

The Two Great Pillars of Boaz and Jachin by Albert G. Mackey & others (978-1-63118-433-8)

Audio Versions are also Available on Audible and iTunes

Table of Contents

Introduction...7

Prologue...9

Part I:
Destruction of the Earth...15

Part II:
The Great Flood...19

Part III:
The First Period of the Angelic Rulers...33

Part IV:
The Second Period...35

Part V:
The Third Period...37

Part VI:
The Fourth Period...39

Part VII:
Judgement of the Fallen Angels...41

Part VIII:
Enoch Wakes From the Dream Visions...45

Introduction

The Apocrypha are a loosely knit series of books, written by early vanguards of Christianity (covering the eras of both the old and new testaments), and which comprise somewhere between about a dozen to several hundred titles, depending on whom you ask and how that person defines "Apocrypha." A small selection of these can still be found included in the Catholic bible, while a majority of the books in question, were abandoned by church officials in the early centuries of Christianity. Many of these apocryphal books were originally considered canon by early followers of Christ, in the first four centuries following his birth. It wasn't until the meeting of the Council of Nicaea in 325, that Emperor Constantine and a group of roughly 300 church bishops, gathered together with the goal of defining, standardizing and unifying an otherwise splintering Christianity, that many of these writings ceased to be included in the newly established canon. Enjoy then, this book as an example, of just one of the many books of the Christian Apocrypha, and be sure to check out other titles in this series.

Prologue

Who is Enoch and why is he so important?

Jude 1:14 describes Enoch as being the seventh generation of man from Adam, while also making reference to Enoch's ability to prophesize. Enoch was born on Seth's side of Adam and Eve's lineage and was the great grandfather of Noah. References to him in the Bible are sparse, but he is most well known for not having died but instead for having walked away with God. In some Christian and Jewish traditions Enoch is also considered to be a scribe and to have been ordained as a priest by Adam.

Perhaps because of Enoch's unique departure from Earth into heaven, there was a rich tradition of exploring what Enoch's life was like, upon leaving Earth. The events of his time in heaven were often explored in classic rabbinical literature as well as the three primary apocryphal books with his name attached to them. Some modern churches continue to embrace Enoch's importance, including the Ethiopian Orthodox Church and perhaps more notably, the Latter Day Saints.

The full text of the magnum opus commonly known as *The Book of Enoch* or *1 Enoch*, is in fact a collection of five separate and unrelated, apocryphal books, the authorship of which spanned several centuries in history, while the real commonality of all being that they each involve Enoch.

The section which is often presented as chapters 83 through 90 of *The Book of Enoch* was originally known as the *Book of Dreams Visions*, or sometimes it was translated as the *Dream Visions of Enoch*. It dates to the mid second century B.C., likely between 163 and 142 B.C. Although, due to the contents of the text itself, oral tradition within the Church often places the writing of this book as having been done prior to the Great Flood, for obvious reasons. This particular translation comes to us from notable scholar of apocryphal literature, R. H. Charles, who published it in 1917.

This book of dreams contains two main visions, although they are very clearly inter-connected. The first one concerns the end of the world, but in a general and overall sense, while the second one is more specific and deals with the universal flood, which eventually leads to the end of the world.

While they *are* two separate dreams, with possible allusions to more, in reality, when you look more closely at them, it would appear that it's more accurate to say that they are multiple parts of a single dream. If we think about our own dreams, most of us can recall a situation where, upon waking from a dream of our own, we attempt to describe to a friend or loved one, a series of multiple but separate, smaller dream sequences, only later realizing that they seem to have collectively morphed into one overall larger dream, somehow, in a way that doesn't make a lot of sense outside of the world of dreams. In this same way, these visions seem to be the account of a single night, so when Enoch is first describing the destruction of the earth and then the flood in a second dream, they are most likely connected.

The dreams of Enoch contain characteristics that lend themselves to a larger symbolic reading. These dreams seem to share the same ancient, cosmographical interpretation of the world, which is outlined in the book of Genesis; and in an overall sense, the book fits in comfortably with other related writings of the time, which exhibit a decidedly apocalyptic nature. In fact, this book could easily be included as part of the tradition referred to as Apocalyptic Literature, a category which usually involves prophecies or visions of the end-times, as revealed by an angel or other heavenly messenger, often told in heavily veiled and colorful symbolism.

Just as we see in books of a similar fashion, given to us from Enoch and others, in this instance, the catalyst for the earth's destruction can be found in the sins of man. The dreams of Enoch are not visions of what *will* come, but instead of what *may* come, if mankind does not change for the better.

The text alternates between Enoch telling his grandfather the events of his vision while asking for advice and Enoch telling his own son the events, after having received advice from his grandfather.

We see Enoch asking God to leave a place for man, after the destruction. The visions, involving different colors of cattle as well as other beasts, would seem to be a retelling of the events of the Books of Genesis and Exodus, but rewritten in the form of a symbolic allegory, such as a one might expect to be found in a dream-vision. Some of these visions can easily be interpreted to line-up with Old Testament events, with regards to the blood lines of Adam and Eve, the events surround the

Israelites, Joseph, Moses and so forth. I would recommend comparing them all side by side, during further contemplation and prayer. In addition to the parallels of different bloodlines, the reader should also be able to see allusions to the events depicted in the narrative of the tower of Babel.

Within the dream, we see black, red and white animals. These three colors are a common trio in the symbology of ancient times, even being incorporated into the Book of Revelations and the four horsemen in that book. They can also be found in various ancient manuscripts, representing the three stages of birth, life and death or of impure, cleansing and pure.

Just as Jesus is often depicted as being a shepherd and the laity are depicted as his flock, this book contains the symbolism of different types of livestock, which is being used to represent humanity, within Enoch's dream.

Without a doubt, all of these types of animals and symbols probably contained much more obvious meaning to the men of ancient times, and the allusions would have been outright obvious. With the passage of time, however, we modern readers are forced to decipher quite a bit and attempt to see through our ancestor's eyes.

As is often the case in these writings, God empowers various angels to rule over mankind, acting as ambassadors, and consequently, we see angels intervening not only to counsel Enoch but to enforce the consequences that were commanded by God but which Enoch can't bring himself to inflict on humanity. As such, toward the end of the book, we see numerous scenes in which angels are ruling over the earth and dealing out punishments, while Enoch is forced to look upon, saddened.

In a simpler fashion, Enoch is relaying the events of his dream, to his son, Methuselah, in a manner to help warn his son of the dangers of going against God. But, Enoch isn't just warning his son, he is also warning us, as we can almost tell in his final words, as he wakes from his dream and weeps.

Part I:

The First Dream-Vision:

Destruction of the Earth

And now, my son Methuselah, I will show thee all my visions which I have seen, recounting them before thee.

Two visions I saw before I took a wife, and the one was quite unlike the other: the first when I was learning to write: the second before I took thy mother, when I saw a terrible vision. And regarding them I prayed to the Lord.

I had laid me down in the house of my grandfather Mahalalel, when I saw in a vision how the heaven collapsed and was borne off and fell to the earth.

And when it fell to the earth I saw how the earth was swallowed up in a great abyss, and mountains were suspended on mountains, and hills sank down on hills, and high trees were rent from their stems, and hurled down and sunk in the abyss.

And thereupon a word fell into my mouth, and I lifted up my voice to cry aloud, and said: *'The earth is destroyed.'*

And my grandfather Mahalalel waked me as I lay near him, and said unto me: *'Why dost thou cry so, my son, and why dost thou make such lamentation?'*

And I recounted to him the whole vision which I had seen, and he said unto me: *'A terrible thing hast thou seen, my son, and of grave moment is thy dream-vision as to the secrets of all the sin of the earth: it must sink into the abyss and be destroyed with a great destruction.*

And now, my son, arise and make petition to the Lord of glory, since thou art a believer, that a remnant may remain on the earth, and that He may not destroy the whole earth.

My son, from heaven all this will come upon the earth, and upon the earth there will be great destruction.'

After that I arose and prayed and implored and besought, and wrote down my prayer for the generations of the world, and I will show everything to thee, my son Methuselah.

And when I had gone forth below and seen the heaven, and the sun rising in the east, and the moon setting in the west, and a few stars, and the whole earth, and everything as He had known it in the beginning, then I blessed the Lord of judgement and extolled Him because He had made the sun to go forth from the windows of the east, and he ascended and rose on the face of the heaven, and set out and kept traversing the path shown unto him.

And I lifted up my hands in righteousness and blessed the Holy and Great One, and spoke with the breath of my mouth, and with the tongue of flesh, which God has made for the children of the flesh of men, that they should speak therewith, and He gave them breath and a tongue and a mouth that they should speak therewith:

'Blessed be Thou, O Lord, King, Great and mighty in Thy greatness, Lord of the whole creation of the heaven, King of kings and God of the whole world.

And Thy power and kingship and greatness abide for ever and ever, And throughout all generations Thy dominion;

And all the heavens are Thy throne for ever, And the whole earth Thy footstool for ever and ever.

For Thou hast made and Thou rulest all things, And nothing is too hard for Thee, Wisdom departs not from the place of Thy throne, Nor turns away from Thy presence.

And Thou knowest and seest and hearest everything, And there is nothing hidden from Thee for Thou seest everything.

And now the angels of Thy heavens are guilty of trespass, And upon the flesh of men abideth Thy wrath until the great day of judgement.

And now, O God and Lord and Great King, I implore and beseech Thee to fulfil my prayer, To leave me a posterity on earth, And not destroy all the flesh of man, And make the earth without inhabitant, So that there should be an eternal destruction.

And now, my Lord, destroy from the earth the flesh which has aroused Thy wrath, But the flesh of righteousness and uprightness establish as a plant of the eternal seed, And hide not Thy face from the prayer of Thy servant, O Lord.'

PART II:

The Second Dream-Vision:

The Great Flood

'And after this I saw another dream, and I will show the whole dream to thee, my son.'

And Enoch lifted up his voice and spoke to his son Methuselah: *'To thee, my son, will I speak: hear my words-- incline thine ear to the dream-vision of thy father.'*

Before I took thy mother Edna, I saw in a vision on my bed, and behold a bull came forth from the earth, and that bull was white; and after it came forth a heifer, and along with this later came forth two bulls, one of them black and the other red.

And that black bull gored the red one and pursued him over the earth, and thereupon I could no longer see that red bull.

But that black bull grew and that heifer went with him, and I saw that many oxen proceeded from him which resembled and followed him.

And that cow, that first one, went from the presence of that first bull in order to seek that red one, but found him not, and lamented with a great lamentation over him and sought him.

And I looked till that first bull came to her and quieted her, and from that time onward she cried no more.

And after that she bore another white bull, and after him she bore many bulls and black cows.

And I saw in my sleep that white bull likewise grow and become a great white bull, and from Him proceeded many white bulls, and they resembled him. And they began to beget many white bulls, which resembled them, one following the other.

And again I saw with mine eyes as I slept, and I saw the heaven above, and behold a star fell from heaven, and it arose and ate and pastured amongst those oxen.

And after that I saw the large and the black oxen, and behold they all changed their stalls and pastures and their cattle, and began to live with each other.

And again I saw in the vision, and looked towards the heaven, and behold I saw many stars descend and cast themselves down from heaven to that first star, and they became bulls amongst those cattle and pastured with them.

And I looked at them and saw, and behold they all let out their privy members, like horses, and began to cover the cows of the oxen, and they all became pregnant and bare elephants, camels, and asses.

And all the oxen feared them and were affrighted at them, and began to bite with their teeth and to devour, and to gore with their horns.

And they began, moreover, to devour those oxen; and behold all the children of the earth began to tremble and quake before them and to flee from them.

And again I saw how they began to gore each other and to devour each other, and the earth began to cry aloud.

And I raised mine eyes again to heaven, and I saw in the vision, and behold there came forth from heaven beings who were like white men: and four went forth from that place and three with them.

And those three that had last come forth grasped me by my hand and took me up, away from the generations of the earth, and raised me up to a lofty place, and showed me a tower raised high above the earth, and all the hills were lower.

And one said unto me: '*Remain here till thou seest everything that befalls those elephants, camels, and asses, and the stars and the oxen, and all of them.*'

And I saw one of those four who had come forth first, and he seized that first star which had fallen from the heaven, and bound it hand and foot and cast it into an abyss: now that abyss was narrow and deep, and horrible and dark.

And one of them drew a sword, and gave it to those elephants and camels and asses: then they began to smite each other, and the whole earth quaked because of them.

And as I was beholding in the vision, lo, one of those four who had come forth, stoned them from heaven, and gathered and took all the great stars whose privy members were like those of horses, and bound them all hand and foot, and cast them in an abyss of the earth.

And one of those four went to that white bull and instructed him in a secret, without his being terrified: he was born a bull and became a man, and built for himself a great vessel and dwelt thereon; and three bulls dwelt with him in that vessel and they were covered in.

And again I raised mine eyes towards heaven and saw a lofty roof, with seven water torrents thereon, and those torrents flowed with much water into an enclosure.

And I saw again, and behold fountains were opened on the surface of that great enclosure, and that water began to swell and rise upon the surface, and I saw that enclosure till all its surface was covered with water.

And the water, the darkness, and mist increased upon it; and as I looked at the height of that water, that water had risen above the height of that enclosure, and was streaming over that enclosure, and it stood upon the earth.

And all the cattle of that enclosure were gathered together until I saw how they sank and were swallowed up and perished in that water.

But that vessel floated on the water, while all the oxen and elephants and camels and asses sank to the bottom with all the animals, so that I could no longer see them, and they were not able to escape, but perished and sank into the depths.

And again I saw in the vision till those water torrents were removed from that high roof, and the chasms of the earth were levelled up and other abysses were opened.

Then the water began to run down into these, till the earth became visible; but that vessel settled on the earth, and the darkness retired and light appeared.

But that white bull which had become a man came out of that vessel, and the three bulls with him, and one of those three was white like that bull, and one of them was red as blood, and one black: and that white bull departed from them.

And they began to bring forth beasts of the field and birds, so that there arose different genera: lions, tigers, wolves, dogs, hyenas, wild boars, foxes, squirrels, swine, falcons, vultures, kites, eagles, and ravens; and among them was born a white bull.

And they began to bite one another; but that white bull which was born amongst them begat a wild ass and a white bull with it, and the wild asses multiplied.

But that bull which was born from him begat a black wild boar and a white sheep; and the former begat many boars, but that sheep begat twelve sheep.

And when those twelve sheep had grown, they gave up one of them to the asses, and those asses again gave up that sheep to the wolves, and that sheep grew up among the wolves.

And the Lord brought the eleven sheep to live with it and to pasture with it among the wolves: and they multiplied and became many flocks of sheep.

And the wolves began to fear them, and they oppressed them until they destroyed their little ones, and they cast their young into a river of much water: but those sheep began to cry aloud on account of their little ones, and to complain unto their Lord.

And a sheep which had been saved from the wolves fled and escaped to the wild asses; and I saw the sheep how they lamented and cried, and besought their Lord with all their might, till that Lord of the sheep descended at the voice of the sheep from a lofty abode, and came to them and pastured them.

And He called that sheep which had escaped the wolves, and spoke with it concerning the wolves that it should admonish them not to touch the sheep.

And the sheep went to the wolves according to the word of the Lord, and another sheep met it and went with it, and the two went and entered together into the assembly of those wolves, and spoke with them and admonished them not to touch the sheep from henceforth.

And thereupon I saw the wolves, and how they oppressed the sheep exceedingly with all their power; and the sheep cried aloud.

And the Lord came to the sheep and they began to smite those wolves: and the wolves began to make lamentation; but the sheep became quiet and forthwith ceased to cry out.

And I saw the sheep till they departed from amongst the wolves; but the eyes of the wolves were blinded, and those wolves departed in pursuit of the sheep with all their power.

And the Lord of the sheep went with them, as their leader, and all His sheep followed Him: and his face was dazzling and glorious and terrible to behold.

But the wolves began to pursue those sheep till they reached a sea of water.

And that sea was divided, and the water stood on this side and on that before their face, and their Lord led them and placed Himself between them and the wolves.

And as those wolves did not yet see the sheep, they proceeded into the midst of that sea, and the wolves followed the sheep, and those wolves ran after them into that sea.

And when they saw the Lord of the sheep, they turned to flee before His face, but that sea gathered itself together, and became as it had been created, and the water swelled and rose till it covered those wolves.

And I saw till all the wolves who pursued those sheep perished and were drowned.

But the sheep escaped from that water and went forth into a wilderness, where there was no water and no grass; and they began to open their eyes and to see; and I saw the Lord of the sheep pasturing them and giving them water and grass, and that sheep going and leading them.

And that sheep ascended to the summit of that lofty rock, and the Lord of the sheep sent it to them.

And after that I saw the Lord of the sheep who stood before them, and His appearance was great and terrible and majestic, and all those sheep saw Him and were afraid before His face.

And they all feared and trembled because of Him, and they cried to that sheep with them which was amongst them: "We are not able to stand before our Lord or to behold Him."

And that sheep which led them again ascended to the summit of that rock, but the sheep began to be blinded and to wander from the way which he had showed them, but that sheep wot not thereof.

And the Lord of the sheep was wrathful exceedingly against them, and that sheep discovered it, and went down from the summit of the rock, and came to the sheep, and found the greatest part of them blinded and fallen away.

And when they saw it they feared and trembled at its presence, and desired to return to their folds.

And that sheep took other sheep with it, and came to those sheep which had fallen away, and began to slay them; and the sheep feared its presence, and thus that sheep brought back those sheep that had fallen away, and they returned to their folds.

And I saw in this vision till that sheep became a man and built a house for the Lord of the sheep, and placed all the sheep in that house.

And I saw till this sheep which had met that sheep which led them fell asleep: and I saw till all the great sheep perished and little ones arose in their place, and they came to a pasture, and approached a stream of water.

Then that sheep, their leader which had become a man, withdrew from them and fell asleep, and all the sheep sought it and cried over it with a great crying.

And I saw till they left off crying for that sheep and crossed that stream of water, and there arose the two sheep as leaders in the place of those which had led them and fallen asleep.

And I saw till the sheep came to a goodly place, and a pleasant and glorious land, and I saw till those sheep were satisfied; and that house stood amongst them in the pleasant land.

And sometimes their eyes were opened, and sometimes blinded, till another sheep arose and led them and brought them all back, and their eyes were opened.

And the dogs and the foxes and the wild boars began to devour those sheep till the Lord of the sheep raised up another sheep a ram from their midst, which led them.

And that ram began to butt on either side those dogs, foxes, and wild boars till he had destroyed them all.

And that sheep whose eyes were opened saw that ram, which was amongst the sheep, till it forsook its glory and began to butt those sheep, and trampled upon them, and behaved itself unseemly.

And the Lord of the sheep sent the lamb to another lamb and raised it to being a ram and leader of the sheep instead of that ram which had forsaken its glory.

And it went to it and spoke to it alone, and raised it to being a ram, and made it the prince and leader of the sheep; but during all these things those dogs oppressed the sheep.

And the first ram pursued that second ram, and that second ram arose and fled before it; and I saw till those dogs pulled down the first ram.

And that second ram arose and led the little sheep.

And those sheep grew and multiplied; but all the dogs, and foxes, and wild boars feared and fled before it, and that ram butted and killed the wild beasts, and those wild beasts had no longer any power among the sheep and robbed them no more of ought.

And that ram begat many sheep and fell asleep; and a little sheep became ram in its stead, and became prince and leader of those sheep.

And that house became great and broad, and it was built for those sheep: and a tower lofty and great was built on the house for the Lord of the sheep, and that house was low, but the tower was elevated and lofty, and the Lord of the sheep stood on that tower and they offered a full table before Him.

And again I saw those sheep that they again erred and went many ways, and forsook that their house, and the Lord of the sheep called some from amongst the sheep and sent them to the sheep, but the sheep began to slay them.

And one of them was saved and was not slain, and it sped away and cried aloud over the sheep; and they sought to slay it, but the Lord of the sheep saved it from the sheep, and brought it up to me, and caused it to dwell there.

And many other sheep He sent to those sheep to testify unto them and lament over them.

And after that I saw that when they forsook the house of the Lord and His tower they fell away entirely, and their eyes were blinded; and I saw the Lord of the sheep how He wrought much slaughter amongst them in their herds until those sheep invited that slaughter and betrayed His place.

And He gave them over into the hands of the lions and tigers, and wolves and hyenas, and into the hand of the foxes, and to all the wild beasts, and those wild beasts began to tear in pieces those sheep.

And I saw that He forsook that their house and their tower and gave them all into the hand of the lions, to tear and devour them, into the hand of all the wild beasts.

And I began to cry aloud with all my power, and to appeal to the Lord of the sheep, and to represent to Him in regard to the sheep that they were devoured by all the wild beasts.

But He remained unmoved, though He saw it, and rejoiced that they were devoured and swallowed and robbed, and left them to be devoured in the hand of all the beasts.

And He called seventy shepherds, and cast those sheep to them that they might pasture them, and He spoke to the shepherds and their companions: *"Let each individual of you pasture the sheep henceforward, and everything that I shall command you that do ye.*

And I will deliver them over unto you duly numbered, and tell you which of them are to be destroyed--and them destroy ye." And He gave over unto them those sheep.

And He called another and spoke unto him: *"Observe and mark everything that the shepherds will do to those sheep; for they will destroy more of them than I have commanded them.*

And every excess and the destruction which will be wrought through the shepherds, record (namely) how many they destroy according to my command, and how many according to their own caprice: record against every individual shepherd all the destruction he effects.

And read out before me by number how many they destroy, and how many they deliver over for destruction, that I may have this as a testimony against them, and know every deed of the shepherds, that I may comprehend and see what they do, whether or not they abide by my command which I have commanded them.

But they shall not know it, and thou shalt not declare it to them, nor admonish them, but only record against each individual all the destruction which the shepherds effect each in his time and lay it all before me."

And I saw till those shepherds pastured in their season, and they began to slay and to destroy more than they were bidden, and they delivered those sheep into the hand of the lions.

And the lions and tigers eat and devoured the greater part of those sheep, and the wild boars eat along with them; and they burnt that tower and demolished that house.

And I became exceedingly sorrowful over that tower because that house of the sheep was demolished, and afterwards I was unable to see if those sheep entered that house.

PART III:

The First Period of the Angelic Rulers

And the shepherds and their associates delivered over those sheep to all the wild beasts, to devour them, and each one of them received in his time a definite number: it was written by the other in a book how many each one of them destroyed of them.

And each one slew and destroyed many more than was prescribed; and I began to weep and lament on account of those sheep.

And thus in the vision I saw that one who wrote, how he wrote down every one that was destroyed by those shepherds, day by day, and carried up and laid down and showed actually the whole book to the Lord of the sheep-- everything that they had done, and all that each one of them had made away with, and all that they had given over to destruction.

And the book was read before the Lord of the sheep, and He took the book from his hand and read it and sealed it and laid it down.

PART IV:

The Second Period

And forthwith I saw how the shepherds pastured for twelve hours, and behold three of those sheep turned back and came and entered and began to build up all that had fallen down of that house; but the wild boars tried to hinder them, but they were not able.

And they began again to build as before, and they reared up that tower, and it was named the high tower; and they began again to place a table before the tower, but all the bread on it was polluted and not pure.

And as touching all this the eyes of those sheep were blinded so that they saw not, and the eyes of their shepherds likewise; and they delivered them in large numbers to their shepherds for destruction, and they trampled the sheep with their feet and devoured them.

And the Lord of the sheep remained unmoved till all the sheep were dispersed over the field and mingled with the beasts, and the shepherds did not save them out of the hand of the beasts.

And this one who wrote the book carried it up, and showed it and read it before the Lord of the sheep, and implored Him on their account, and besought Him on their account as he showed Him all the doings of the shepherds, and gave testimony before Him against all the shepherds. And he took the actual book and laid it down beside Him and departed.

PART V:

The Third Period

And I saw till that in this manner thirty-five shepherds undertook the pasturing of the sheep, and they severally completed their periods as did the first; and others received them into their hands, to pasture them for their period, each shepherd in his own period.

And after that I saw in my vision all the birds of heaven coming, the eagles, the vultures, the kites, the ravens; but the eagles led all the birds; and they began to devour those sheep, and to pick out their eyes and to devour their flesh.

And the sheep cried out because their flesh was being devoured by the birds, and as for me I looked and lamented in my sleep over that shepherd who pastured the sheep.

And I saw until those sheep were devoured by the dogs and eagles and kites, and they left neither flesh nor skin nor sinew remaining on them till only their bones stood there: and their bones too fell to the earth and the sheep became few.

And I saw until that twenty-three had undertaken the pasturing and completed in their several periods fifty-eight times.

PART VI:

The Fourth Period

But behold lambs were borne by those white sheep, and they began to open their eyes and to see, and to cry to the sheep.

Yea, they cried to them, but they did not hearken to what they said to them, but were exceedingly deaf, and their eyes were very exceedingly blinded.

And I saw in the vision how the ravens flew upon those lambs and took one of those lambs, and dashed the sheep in pieces and devoured them.

And I saw till horns grew upon those lambs, and the ravens cast down their horns; and I saw till there sprouted a great horn of one of those sheep, and their eyes were opened.

And it looked at them and their eyes opened, and it cried to the sheep, and the rams saw it and all ran to it.

And notwithstanding all this those eagles and vultures and ravens and kites still kept tearing the sheep and swooping down upon them and devouring them: still the sheep remained silent, but the rams lamented and cried out.

And those ravens fought and battled with it and sought to lay low its horn, but they had no power over it.

And I saw till the shepherds and eagles and those vultures and kites came, and they cried to the ravens that they should break the horn of that ram, and they battled and fought with it, and it battled with them and cried that its help might come.

And I saw till a great sword was given to the sheep, and the sheep proceeded against all the beasts of the field to slay them, and all the beasts and the birds of the heaven fled before their face.

And I saw that man, who wrote the book according to the command of the Lord, till he opened that book concerning the destruction which those twelve last shepherds had wrought, and showed that they had destroyed much more than their predecessors, before the Lord of the sheep.

And I saw till the Lord of the sheep came unto them and took in His hand the staff of His wrath, and smote the earth, and the earth clave asunder, and all the beasts and all the birds of the heaven fell from among those sheep, and were swallowed up in the earth and it covered them.

PART VII:

Judgements of the Fallen Angels

And I saw till a throne was erected in the pleasant land, and the Lord of the sheep sat Himself thereon, and the other took the sealed books and opened those books before the Lord of the sheep.

And the Lord called those men the seven first white ones, and commanded that they should bring before Him, beginning with the first star which led the way, all the stars whose privy members were like those of horses, and they brought them all before Him.

And He said to that man who wrote before Him, being one of those seven white ones, and said unto him: *"Take those seventy shepherds to whom I delivered the sheep, and who taking them on their own authority slew more than I commanded them."*

And behold they were all bound, I saw, and they all stood before Him.

And the judgement was held first over the stars, and they were judged and found guilty, and went to the place of condemnation, and they were cast into an abyss, full of fire and flaming, and full of pillars of fire.

And those seventy shepherds were judged and found guilty, and they were cast into that fiery abyss.

And I saw at that time how a like abyss was opened in the midst of the earth, full of fire, and they brought those blinded sheep, and they were all judged and found guilty and cast into this fiery abyss, and they burned; now this abyss was to the right of that house.

And I saw those sheep burning and their bones burning.

And I stood up to see till they folded up that old house; and carried off all the pillars, and all the beams and ornaments of the house were at the same time folded up with it, and they carried it off and laid it in a place in the south of the land.

And I saw till the Lord of the sheep brought a new house greater and loftier than that first, and set it up in the place of the first which had been folded up: all its pillars were new, and its ornaments were new and larger than those of the first, the old one which He had taken away, and all the sheep were within it.

And I saw all the sheep which had been left, and all the beasts on the earth, and all the birds of the heaven, falling down and doing homage to those sheep and making petition to and obeying them in everything.

And thereafter those three who were clothed in white and had seized me by my hand, and the hand of that ram also seizing hold of me, they took me up and set me down in the midst of those sheep before the judgement took place.

And those sheep were all white, and their wool was abundant and clean.

And all that had been destroyed and dispersed, and all the beasts of the field, and all the birds of the heaven, assembled in that house, and the Lord of the sheep rejoiced with great joy because they were all good and had returned to His house.

And I saw till they laid down that sword, which had been given to the sheep, and they brought it back into the house, and it was sealed before the presence of the Lord, and all the sheep were invited into that house, but it held them not.

And the eyes of them all were opened, and they saw the good, and there was not one among them that did not see.

And I saw that that house was large and broad and very full.

And I saw that a white bull was born, with large horns and all the beasts of the field and all the birds of the air feared him and made petition to him all the time.

And I saw till all their generations were transformed, and they all became white bulls; and the first among them became a lamb, and that lamb became a great animal and had great black horns on its head; and the Lord of the sheep rejoiced over it and over all the oxen.

And I slept in their midst.

PART VIII:

Enoch Wakes From the Dream Visions

And then, I awoke and saw everything.

This is the vision which I saw while I slept, and I awoke and blessed the Lord of righteousness and gave Him glory.

Then I wept with a great weeping and my tears stayed not till I could no longer endure it: when I saw, they flowed on account of what I had seen; for everything shall come and be fulfilled, and all the deeds of men in their order were shown to me.

On that night I remembered the first dream, and because of it I wept and was troubled--because I had seen that vision.

www.ingramcontent.com/pod-product-compliance
Lightning Source LLC
LaVergne TN
LVHW041501070426
835507LV00009B/748